Year of the Horse

To Lifen Zhang and Jiewei Cheng N.S.

For Nick, Janis and Sophie W.A.

馬年

Year of the Horse

PAVILION

First published in Great Britain in 2002 by
PAVILION BOOKS LIMITED
64 Brewery Road
London N7 9NT
www.pavilionbooks.co.uk

A member of the Chrysalis Group plc

Designed by Wherefore Art?

A CIP catalogue record for this book is available
from the British Library.

ISBN 1 86205 472 X

Set in BauerBodoni and Linoscript
Colour reproduction by Bright Arts, Singapore
Printed and bound by Imago, Singapore

2 4 6 8 10 9 7 5 3 1

This book can be ordered direct from the publisher. Please contact
the Marketing Department. But try your bookshop first.

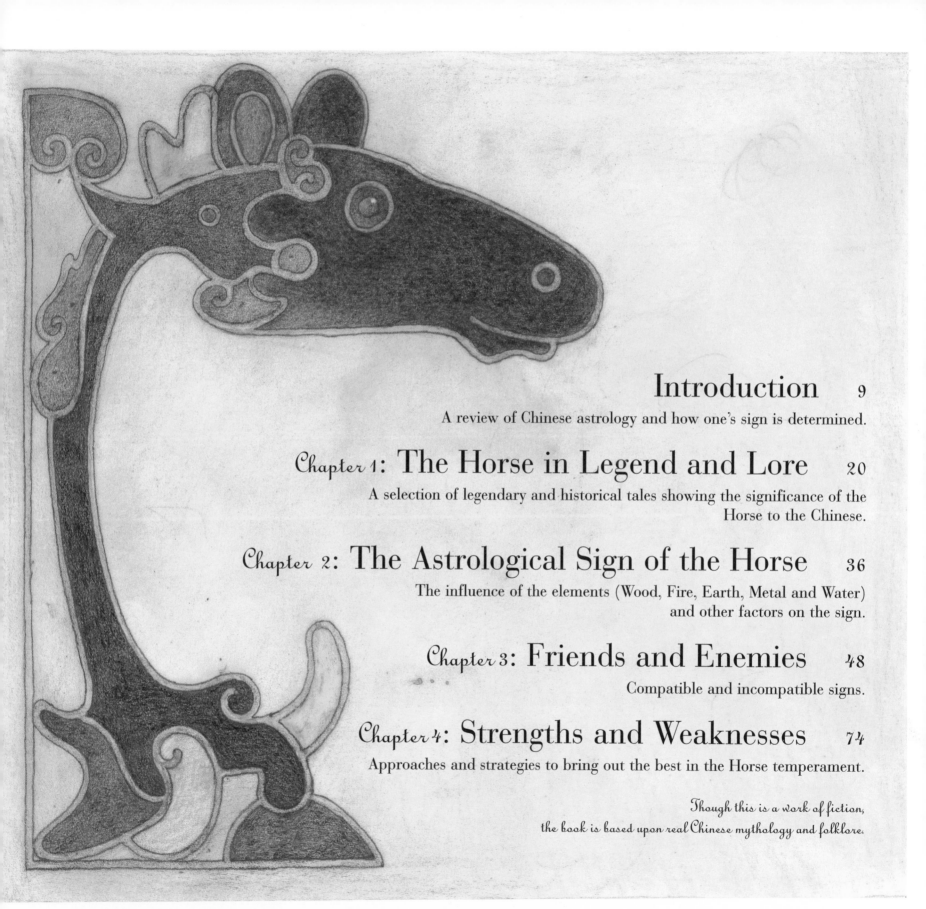

Though this is a work of fiction,
the book is based upon real Chinese mythology and folklore.

Editor's Note

THIS JOURNAL IS A COLLECTION OF HORSE LEGEND AND LORE - COMBINING MYTHOLOGY, FOLK TALE AND CLASSIC LITERATURE. THIS ILLUMINATING GUIDE EXPLORES WHAT CHINESE ASTROLOGY HAS TO SAY ABOUT PEOPLE BORN UNDER THE SIGN OF THE HORSE; GIVING THOSE WITH NO PREVIOUS KNOWLEDGE OF THE SUBJECT A PRACTICAL MEANS OF FINDING OUT THEIR OWN ASTROLOGICAL PROFILE.

It follows the chance discovery of another journal in a Suffolk auction in 1998 apparently by an English traveller in China in the late eighteenth century. After slight editing this was published under the title *Year of the Dragon* and the welcome it received prompted further investigations. We learned little more about the author, beyond that she was female, but by chance we stumbled in our search upon a whole pile of further journals by the same hand(s), a treasure trove of belief from just before the great upheavals in Chinese culture. The sources are usually traceable to classic books and folktales that are still in circulation today.

For modern readers we have revised the original outline of how to determine one's birth profile, but otherwise have mostly just let the journal speak for itself. The author's magpie-like approach to gathering information often seems haphazard, but that is part of the journal's charm and there is often more logic than appears at first sight.

The result is a survey of the horse's traditional place in Chinese astrology and culture, the myths and legends surrounding it and a guide to seeing where you personally fit into it all. We have tidied up the text slightly to make it more palatable to modern readers, but nothing significant has been added. To preserve the flavour, certain names such as Peking and Genghis Khan have been kept in the familiar form the author employs, but otherwise we have used modern Pin Yin wherever possible.

Introduction

Determining your Birth Sign

THE FIRST THING ANYONE EVEN MILDLY CURIOUS ABOUT CHINESE ASTROLOGY WILL WANT TO KNOW IS HIS OR HER OVERALL BIRTH SIGN. LUCKILY, NOTHING COULD BE SIMPLER BECAUSE IN CHINESE ASTROLOGY THIS IS DECIDED SIMPLY BY THE YEAR IN WHICH YOU WERE BORN. THE MONTH, DAY AND HOUR ALSO PLAY THEIR PARTS, BUT THE YEAR IS PARAMOUNT. THE ONLY COMPLICATION IS THAT THE CHINESE NEW YEAR VARIES, LIKE EASTER, FROM YEAR TO YEAR, BEING TIMED BY THE SECOND NEW MOON AFTER THE SHORTEST DAY OF THE YEAR.

For a full list of years and signs see the table on page 14, but the Horse is your sign if you were born between the dates below.

11 February 1918 – 1 February 1919

30 January 1930 – 17 February 1931

15 February 1942 – 5 February 1943

3 February 1954 – 24 January 1955

21 January 1966 – 9 February 1967

7 February 1978 – 28 January 1979

27 January 1990 – 15 February 1991

12 February 2002 – 1 February 2003

As everyone born in a particular year shares the same sign, the Chinese are far more coy than Westerners about revealing their sign to strangers because it immediately reveals their age – unless they happen to look twelve years younger than they are. However, any doubt on this score can be resolved by delicately checking what element their sign is, because although each sign recurs every twelve years, it is coloured by each of the five elements in turn. So it is in fact sixty years before any sign recurs in exactly the same form. When people reach the age of sixty in China they hold a special celebration to mark having passed through a complete cycle. All of the following years are

considered a bounty and the opinions of the elderly are listened to with a special respect because they have experienced a complete round of the cosmic clock. This period is the basis of all Chinese chronology and is known as the Heavenly Year, or *Tai Sui*, which is also their name for astrology, and was established by the legendary Emperor Huang Di in 2637 BC. All major events in Chinese history since then can be fixed quite precisely by his calendar.

Having everyone born in a year share the same astrological sign may seem a sweeping generalization. Sceptics will argue that it is far too broad a generalization, even more so than in Western astrology. But what Chinese astrologers are claiming is simply that we are more affected by the year of our birth than by any other factor, which is quite reasonable, even without thinking in terms of astrology. An eighty-year-old will always view the past and present very differently to a twenty-year-old, even if in other respects they appear identical. We are all moulded by our experiences and the spirit of the times in which we evolve, so the year of our birth will have an enormous impact, whatever our individual natures.

Chinese astrology goes much further than this, however. It aims to define precisely the character of each year in symbolic terms. And when it then moves on to consider the influence of the month, day and hour of birth, it comes very close to Western astrology in giving each person a unique blueprint for life.

Luckily for our understanding of the system, the totem animals that the Chinese assign to the months, days, hours (and even minutes if you want to take it that far), are identical to those applied to the years. There is no need to master a new set of symbols for each level. Just grasp what the twelve main totems represent and, to a degree, you can be your own astrologer. The beauty of the Chinese system is that it is so simple to learn the basics and get a general picture of what it has to say about you; but it can be taken a lot further.

Besides your year sign, you also have a month sign in Chinese astrology, which corresponds closely to one of the twelve periods of the Western zodiac.

Many people even prefer to take this as their 'true' Chinese horoscope sign, and they are perfectly entitled to do so if they feel more comfortable with it. There is nothing in Chinese astrology to forbid it – and possibly it better suits the more individualistic temper of the West – but the Chinese might say you are missing the main picture. To them, your year sign is your Yang or 'outgoing aspect'. It is the face you show to the world in business dealings, say. Your month sign is your Yin aspect. It is the character you display in personal relationships, in one to one dealings with others.

Month Sign

RAT – SAGITTARIUS

OX – CAPRICORN

TIGER – AQUARIUS

HARE – PISCES

DRAGON – ARIES

SNAKE – TAURUS

HORSE – GEMINI

GOAT – CANCER

MONKEY – LEO

ROOSTER – VIRGO

DOG – LIBRA

BOAR – SCORPIO

Most people can find their Chinese month sign simply by glancing at the equivalents above. However, if your birthday falls near the limits of your Western star sign you need a simple calculation to be sure. This is because the date upon which the Chinese New Year commences varies from year to year.

To determine your Chinese month sign, first look up the date of the New Year before your birthday in the table on page 14. This marks the opening of the month of the Tiger. The same date in the

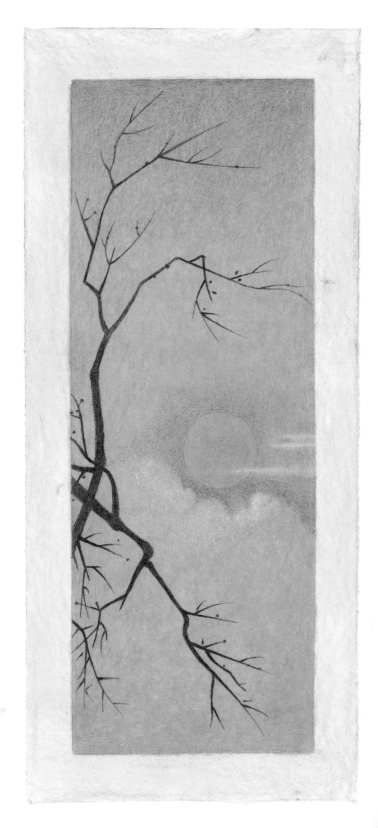

following month (by Western reckoning) opens the month of the Hare, and so on through the cycle of signs until you reach your birthday. The last month in the cycle is that of the Ox, whose length varies considerably depending on the date of the following New Year.

For example: in 1978 the Chinese New Year fell on 7 February. So the month of the Tiger ran from 7 February to 7 March, the Hare until 7 April, the Dragon until 7 May, the Snake until 7 June, and so on. If you were born on 16 April that year, your monthly sign would be the Dragon. 1978 was a Year of the Horse, therefore, in Chinese astrology you are a Dragon-Horse. In personal relationships you behave as a Dragon while to the wider world you are a Horse.

The day of your birth also has a character but the calculations are too impractical to go into here, considering the relatively small impact it has on your profile. The hour of birth, however, is both significant and easy to assign if you happen to know it.

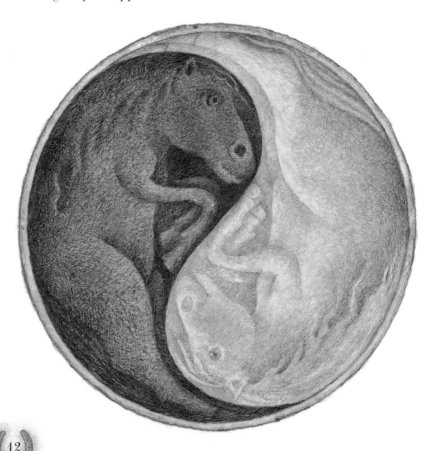

Hour Sign

The two factors we have so far, the year and month signs, are enough to tell a great deal about a person, but the sign associated with the hour of birth can give the key to understanding a character. Often called the 'Secret' or 'Hidden Sign', it reveals how we feel in our innermost selves.

The Chinese day, like the year, is divided into twelve periods governed by the astrological signs, each two-hour period having a Yang and a Yin half. If you know your time of birth, check the table below to see what your hour sign is.

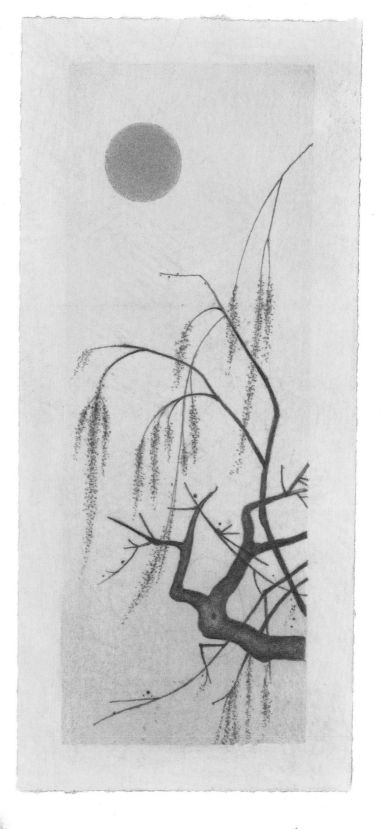

	YANG	YIN
RAT	11pm – 12	12 – 1am
OX	1am – 2am	2am – 3am
TIGER	3am – 4am	4am – 5am
HARE	5am – 6am	6am – 7am
DRAGON	7am – 8am	8am – 9am
SNAKE	9am – 10am	10am – 11am
HORSE	11am – 12	12 – 1pm
GOAT	1pm – 2pm	2pm – 3pm
MONKEY	3pm – 4pm	4pm – 5pm
ROOSTER	5pm – 6pm	6pm – 7pm
DOG	7pm – 8pm	8pm – 9pm
BOAR	9pm – 10pm	10pm – 11pm

Taking once again the example of 16 April 1978: if you were born at 11.30am this would mean that your inner sign is a Yang Horse, perfectly matching your year. But if you were born the preceding midnight, your hour sign would be the Rat, which could create interesting tensions because the Rat and the Horse tend to loathe each other.

RAT	OX	TIGER	HARE	DRAGON	SNAKE	HORSE	GOAT	MONKEY	ROOSTER	DOG	BOAR
					Year:	1930	1931	1932	1933	1934	1935
			Chinese New Year begins on:			30 Jan	17 Feb	6 Feb	26 Jan	14 Feb	4 Feb
			Element associated with that year:			Metal	Metal	Water	Water	Wood	Wood
1936	1937	1938	1939	1940	1941	1942	1943	1944	1945	1946	1947
24 Jan	11 Feb	31 Jan	19 Feb	8 Feb	27 Jan	15 Feb	5 Feb	25 Jan	13 Feb	2 Feb	22 Jan
Fire	Fire	Earth	Earth	Metal	Metal	Water	Water	Wood	Wood	Fire	Fire
1948	1949	1950	1951	1952	1953	1954	1955	1956	1957	1958	1959
8 Feb	29 Jan	17 Feb	6 Feb	27 Jan	14 Feb	3 Feb	24 Jan	12 Feb	31 Jan	18 Feb	8 Feb
Earth	Earth	Metal	Metal	Water	Water	Wood	Wood	Fire	Fire	Earth	Earth
1960	1961	1962	1963	1964	1965	1966	1967	1968	1969	1970	1971
28 Jan	15 Feb	5 Feb	25 Jan	13 Feb	2 Feb	21 Jan	9 Feb	30 Jan	17 Feb	6 Feb	27 Jan
Metal	Metal	Water	Water	Wood	Wood	Fire	Fire	Earth	Earth	Metal	Metal
1972	1973	1974	1975	1976	1977	1978	1979	1980	1981	1982	1983
16 Feb	3 Feb	23 Jan	11 Feb	31 Jan	18 Feb	7 Feb	28 Jan	16 Feb	5 Feb	25 Jan	13 Feb
Water	Water	Wood	Wood	Fire	Fire	Earth	Earth	Metal	Metal	Water	Water
1984	1985	1986	1987	1988	1989	1990	1991	1992	1993	1994	1995
2 Feb	20 Feb	9 Feb	29 Jan	17 Feb	6 Feb	27 Jan	15 Feb	4 Feb	23 Jan	10 Feb	31 Jan
Wood	Wood	Fire	Fire	Earth	Earth	Metal	Metal	Water	Water	Wood	Wood
1996	1997	1998	1999	2000	2001	2002	2003	2004	2005	2006	2007
19 Feb	8 Feb	28 Jan	16 Feb	5 Feb	24 Jan	12 Feb	1 Feb	22 Jan	9 Feb	29 Jan	18 Feb
Fire	Fire	Earth	Earth	Metal	Metal	Water	Water	Wood	Wood	Fire	Fire
2008	2009	2010	2011	2022	2013	2014					
7 Feb	26 Jan	14 Feb	3 Feb	23 Jan	10 Feb	31 Jan					
Earth	Earth	Metal	Metal	Water	Water	Wood					

Now you have a profile of yourself in Chinese astrological terms. But what does it all mean? Well, that should become clear in time, but first let's enter the journal proper, beginning with the author's own introduction. Remember that it appears to be written at the end of the eighteenth century, when the Manchu dynasty was still flourishing and the Chinese had little idea that their ancient way of life was about to be shaken to the roots by contact with Europe and America. The author was most likely the wife of a diplomat, missionary or businessman on tour.

It is impossible for me to overstate the importance of astrology in all aspects of Chinese life, from buying a chicken coop to the very highest decisions of state.

No crops will be planted or wedding even be contemplated without first hiring an astrologer to search the charts for a propitious date. Before a couple may wed, they must even prove to their families that their birth signs are in harmony.

So pervasive is this belief, that to be an astrologer in China is a highly honoured profession, akin to that of a doctor or civil servant. There are of course charlatans to be found, as in any profession, but the rest appear to have earned their places in society by giving at least the impression of sound advice.

Whether or not one believes in astrology, we found it impossible to ignore, especially during our early travels through the Shantung and Chih-li [Hopei] Provinces. Our Western sensibilities were at first bemused by the seriousness with which the subject is taken. At home, astrology is at best a kind of parlour game taken only half seriously, if at all. It is viewed as a quaint relic of ancient superstition. But here in China even the highest government officials, men of the greatest intellectual rigour, will solemnly insist on consulting the heavens before confirming any major decision, or setting a date for its execution.

The emperor told his officers that among other signs which would enable them to fix the exact period of the year's cardinal points, the spring equinox might be determined by observing the star Neaou, the summer solstice by observing the star Ho, the autumn equinox by observing the star Heu, and the winter solstice by observing the star Maou.

SHU JING, BOOK 1

Indeed, the advice we received from astrologers ourselves on several occasions was so startling in its accuracy that we were drawn to look closer into it. Most rewarding this turned out to be, too, because astrology is a window into the Chinese soul. Having gradually developed since the greatest antiquity, it has absorbed along the way all the deepest beliefs and dreams of its makers.

So important was astrology deemed in ancient times that the Emperor Yao, over 2000 years before the birth of our Lord, established the tradition of Imperial Astrologers. He appointed two, named Xi and Ho, and placed them among his chief advisers. The *Shu Jing* or *Book of History*, one of the five classics of Chinese literature, records that Yao ordered them to 'Observe the heavens, calculate and define the courses of the sun, moon and stars and the zodiacal spaces, and so, respectfully, to deliver the seasons to the people.'

Xi and Ho were the names of the original astrologers, but they seem to have become the titles of their successors, because some 200 years later, Emperor Chuang Kung, the third of the Xia dynasty, beheaded his astrologers, also called Xi and Ho, for failing to predict a solar eclipse and the panic this caused. As it says in the *Shih Jing* or *Records of the Grand Historian* by Sima Qian.

'Xi and Ho, being drunk with wine, made no use of their talents. Without respect for their obligations to the prince, they abandoned their office and were the first who disturbed the good order of the calendar, whose care had been entrusted to them. For on the first day of the last moon of autumn, the sun and moon being in conjunction and conflict in Fang [the constellation Scorpio], the blind one beat the drum, the mandarins mounted their steeds, and the people ran about in fear. At that time Xi and Ho, like wooden statues, neither saw nor heard anything, and by their negligence in calculating and observing the movement of the stars, they invoked the penalty of death promulgated by our earlier princes.'

Since the nation's fortune was believed to depend totally on that of the emperor, the stars regulated his life more than anyone else's. As the

Year of the Horse

embodiment of his people, whose whims could affect the lives of millions, the emperor's every move was designed with the greatest care to be in harmony with the flow of the universe – as revealed by astrology in relation to his birth chart. So the grasp of time was seen as a tool of government as well as of agriculture, and thus it was essential to be able to fix times and dates accurately.

So it was believed anyway, and still seems to be believed today in China. Many different forms of timekeeping were tried through the ages but Emperor Shen Tsung of the Song dynasty, who ruled circa AD 1100, deemed none satisfactory. He determined to build the most perfect clock the world had yet seen; and entrusted the project to one of his ministers, Su Sung, an ambassador with scientific leanings. Su Sung assembled a team of the greatest minds in the Empire and in two years they built the basic wooden timekeeping mechanism. After two more years the armillary spheres and dials had been added, for this clock was not only meant to count the hours of the day, but to mark the month, season and year as well, besides tracing the courses of the sun, moon and stars. On completion it stood forty feet tall and was finally presented to the emperor with a manual describing how it had been built and how it worked. Copies of this book are said to be still in circulation today, though we were unable to lay hands on one.

Su Sung's clock seems to have been impelled by a waterwheel whose turning was regulated by a catchment device similar to those of modern clocks. It was the wonder of its age and people came from all over the Empire to admire it. But it does not seem to have been as accurate as everyone had hoped. Yeh Meng-te tells us in his histories how the emperor once sent Su Sung with a winter solstice gift for a Tartar ruler in the north. To the embarrassment of the Empire he arrived a day late, having timed the journey by his own clock. With refreshing candour Su Sung confessed to the emperor on his return that the barbarians could still measure time more accurately by the stars alone. However, his clock remained probably the finest in the world until the Tartars destroyed it some thirty years later, and the art of clock making was extinguished in China for centuries.

民間傳奇中兩馬

Chapter One

The Horse in Legend and Lore

HORSES ARE THE MILITARY READINESS OF THE STATE.

IF HEAVEN REMOVES THAT READINESS, THE STATE WILL TOTTER AND FALL.

BOOK OF TANG, EIGHTH CENTURY

Horses have always been highly prized in China both for their own sakes and as tokens of wealth and strength. In the ancient histories, kingdoms are often measured more in terms of how many horses and chariots they could muster than the size or population of the realm.

This is because China has always been threatened and often overrun by irrepressible 'barbarian' hordes thundering out of the steppes and deserts of the north-west on horseback – Huns, Mongols, Tartars, Manchurians… Emperor Shi Huang Di built the Great Wall around the time of Our Lord to hold them back, but the fate of Chinese dynasties still rested largely on their cavalry. One emperor after another decreed vastly expensive breeding programs to try and improve the quality of their horses, and the silk trade with the West developed largely in order to buy in fresh breeding stock, often from the very enemies against whom the Chinese were trying to defend themselves.

This ancient dependence on the horse for safety explains the Chinese estimation of the creature in daily life. Although riders all around the world take pride in their horses, in China there is an added dimension to this.

TERRACOTTA FIGURES FROM THE TOMB OF SHI HUANG DI, THE UNIFIER OF CHINA WHOSE BRIEF QIN (CHIN) DYNASTY GAVE THE COUNTRY ITS NAME.

HORSE STATUE FROM A TANG DYNASTY GRAVE OF THE EIGHTH CENTURY AD.

RECORDS FROM THAT TIME SHOW THAT THE EMPEROR COULD CALL ON OVER 700,000 HORSES TO DEFEND HIS REALM. IN THE EARLIEST DAYS KINGS' HORSES WERE SACRIFICED AND BURIED WITH THEM (ALONG WITH WIVES, SLAVES AND MANY OTHER LIVING BEINGS). THIS WAS NOT ONLY FOR COMPANY IN THE AFTERLIFE BUT PROTECTION AGAINST DEMONS, WHO ARE TERRIFIED OF HORSES BECAUSE THEY ARE THE OFFICIAL BEARERS OF SOULS TO THE UNDERWORLD AND THE DEPUTIES OF ITS AWESOME RULER, THE YAMA KING. MINDFUL OF THIS, MANY PEOPLE AT NEW YEAR MAKE CAREFUL OFFERINGS OF SWEETS TO THE JADE EMPEROR OF HEAVEN'S HORSE IN THE HOPE THAT IT WILL PUT A GOOD WORD IN FOR THEM WHEN THEIR TIME COMES. LATER ON, IT WAS DECIDED THAT SACRIFICES OF LIVING HORSES WERE UNNECESSARY AND RULERS SATISFIED THEMSELVES WITH STATUES INSTEAD, WHICH WERE BELIEVED ABLE TO COME ALIVE AT NIGHT TO ATTACK GRAVE ROBBERS.

On the Frontier

A Tartar horn tugs at the north wind
The Thistle Gate shines brighter than the stream
The sky swallows the road to Kokonor
On the Great Wall a thousand miles of moonlight.

The dew descends on to damp banners
Cold bronze chimes the watches of the night
The barbarians' armour meshes like serpent scales
Horses whinny and the Evergreen Mound is champed bare.

In the still of autumn, see the flickering Pleiades
Far out on the sands, warning of danger in the gorse
North of the barbarians' tents is surely the sky's ending
Where the river's ripple streams beyond the border.

LI HO, TANG DYNASTY C. AD 800

In Chinese astrology the horse is not primarily a mystical creature. In fact, with the exception of the dragon, none of the twelve symbolic beasts are, because the creatures of the zodiac are totem animals taken from daily life in the countryside. Many Chinese would even dispute the mythical status of the dragon because they believe as firmly in its reality as in any of the others. The creatures were chosen (by the Buddha himself, it is said) because they were creatures that everyone could relate to; even if, as with the tiger and snake, they were not beasts that anyone particularly wanted to meet

every day. The creatures represent different aspects of the universe in general and human behaviour in particular. Several of them do play a lively role in supernatural tales, but it is their everyday aspect that one should mainly bear in mind when trying to grasp what they represent in astrology.

Nevertheless, any mystical association the animals have adds colour to people's perception of them. And with the horse there is an immediate link with one of the most wonderful of all creatures in Chinese

The Horse in Legend & Lore

mythology, the unicorn or *Qi Lin*. Legend declares that this was among the four Most Fortunate Beasts that came first into existence at the creation of the world, along with the dragon, phoenix and tortoise.

Like our Western unicorn it is the gentlest of creatures and the friend of all others. It is said to walk in the daintiest possible manner to avoid treading on insects and its voice is like the sweet chiming of a bell. It is very rarely seen but makes an auspicious appearance at the birth of great emperors and sages, and then again as a mark of respect when they die. If there are no reports of a Qi Lin being sighted when a new emperor takes the Dragon Throne, people fear the worst.

One of the clearest descriptions of the unicorn appears in a fragment of the *Bamboo Books* which we came across by chance in the market at Kow-ling, where we were staying at the mission:

The Qi Lin springs from the earth's central regions. It is endowed with goodness, possessing the body of a horse; the tail of an ox; the feet of a deer and one horn, the tip of which is fleshy. It rambles only on selected grounds and only then after it has examined the locality. It will not live in herds or be accompanied in its movements. It cannot be beguiled into pitfalls or captured in snares. When the king is virtuous, this beast appears. It is the chief of all the 360 kinds of hairy creature.

A Qi Lin or 'dragon-horse' is supposed in legend to have appeared to the divine Emperor Fu Xi about 5,000 years ago, rising from the waters of the Yellow River. On its back were eight markings made up of broken and unbroken lines. These became the eight *Ba Gua*, the foundation of both Chinese divination and writing.

The Taoist Immortal, Chang Kuo, one of the eight who gained eternal life while still in the flesh, is purported to have won his immortality by chasing a unicorn to the moon where it changed into a peach, which he ate. Chang Kuo (or possibly one of the other Immortals) also possessed a marvellous milk-white flying horse that could be folded up like a piece of paper and carried around in his purse. Chang Kuo and the rest are the subject of countless, often comical, folk stories told around the country by Buddhists and Taoists alike.

In the fifth century BC a Qi Lin heralded the birth of Confucius, China's greatest sage. It is told that his mother, Chang-tsai, had a vision while she was pregnant in which she was visited by a Qi Lin accompanied by five elders who introduced themselves as the gods of the major planets. Other versions of the tale say she was on her way to a mountain shrine to pray for fertility, as her husband Heh was old and desperate to see an heir before he went to heaven. Either way, the Qi Lin knelt before Chang-tsai and dropped from its mouth a jade tablet bearing the inscription: 'The son of the essence of water shall succeed the decaying Zhou [dynasty] and be a king without a throne.' Chang-tsai tied a ribbon about its horn before the creature left and then pondered the prophecy.

'A king without a throne' proved the best possible description of Confucius because during his life he never held seriously high office or persuaded any prince to fully implement all his ideas, but after death they became the principles by which the Empire has been governed almost ever since.

Confucius' philosophy was highly practical and down to earth. Living in the period known as the Warring States, his main concern was good government and correct behaviour in everyday life. He did spend years studying and adding to the ancient *I Qing* or *Book of Changes*, and accepted its mystical premises. In fact, he wished he could have spent much more time on it because to him it seemed to contain all wisdom, but otherwise he refused to be drawn into speculation about dragons, gods or anything else of which he had no first-hand experience. Yet he seems never to have doubted the reality of unicorns, perhaps because of the tale of his birth.

Towards the end of Confucius' life in the spring of 481 BC some hunters (or wood-gatherers in other versions) accidentally killed a strange and unfamiliar creature. They sent for Confucius who immediately recognized it as a Qi Lin. According to the chronicle of Kung-yang he cried out: 'The Qi Lin, the Qi Lin, for whom have you come?' Then, 'The course of my teaching is run.' And although he was to live another two years, he brought a swift end to the *Spring and Autumn Annals* that he was then writing and laid down his pen to await his end.

Thus, in Chinese astrology the horse immediately conjures echoes of the unicorn but less so than in Europe or America, because although the Qi Lin is most often described as resembling a horse with a single horn, elsewhere it is likened to a deer or a cow or even an ox.

A stronger link between horses and the divine might be found in the legend of Khun, the third emperor of pre-dynastic China, who had supernatural powers and often took the form of a white horse. Khun is most famous for his battles against the floods that in his day threatened to drown the world. First, he tried building dams, but when they collapsed he stole some magical 'Swelling Earth' from heaven, which for the Chinese exists in the constellation of the Plough. This magic substance tamed the floods but the Emperor of Heaven was furious at the theft. He despatched his executioner who

CONFUCIUS

slew Khun for his presumption on Feather Mountain. There his body lay incorrupt for three years till his belly was cut open with a sword and his son Yu was miraculously born as a rare winged dragon. Yu continued his father's war against the floods but wisely asked permission before taking any more of the magical Swelling Earth. Yu mastered the floods by raising mountains above them and carving out river-courses with his dragon tail; he then became emperor himself and founded the first dynasty, the Xia.

Another supernatural association might be with Ma-mian (Horse-face). Along with Niu-tou (Ox-head) this goddess is the chief attendant of each district's deity or *Cheng-huang*. The Cheng-huang is usually a local hero who has been spared reincarnation by the Emperor of Heaven so that he can continue to protect his homeland. Each spring the Cheng-huang's statue is carried in procession around the territory accompanied by statues of, or people dressed up as, Ma-mian and Niu-tou.

Ma-mian and Niu-tou also guard the district against demons and lead souls of the dead to the Cheng-huang for preliminary judgement. He keeps them for forty-nine days, during which time they are allowed to argue if they feel they have died too soon. If they win their case, they are allowed to return to life; for which reason bodies are often not buried until the end of the period. After forty-nine days, the Cheng-huang hands the souls over to the lord of the underworld for more thorough judgement.

Silkworm breeding is under the protection of the Lady Horse-head. The story goes that she was once mortal, the daughter of a seafaring

LADY HORSE-HEAD

merchant. When pirates kidnapped her father, the girl pined away. Her mother, in despair, swore aloud to the gods that she would give her daughter in marriage to any person who brought her husband home. Now, the girl had a horse gifted with intelligence and the power of speech – a human who'd had a spell cast on him by a wizard. This horse overheard the mother's vow and, having long been in love with his mistress, determined to win the prize. He set off and after many adventures brought her father safely home. Everyone was overjoyed until the horse opened its mouth and demanded his reward. The girl's father was outraged by this impudence and immediately killed the horse for its presumption. It was then flayed and the skin hung out on a fence to dry. That seemed the end of the matter and although the girl was sad about the horse, she could not blame her father too much after his terrible ordeals. Three days later, as she passed the fence where the horse's hide was tanning in the sun, it leaped off and wrapped itself around her,

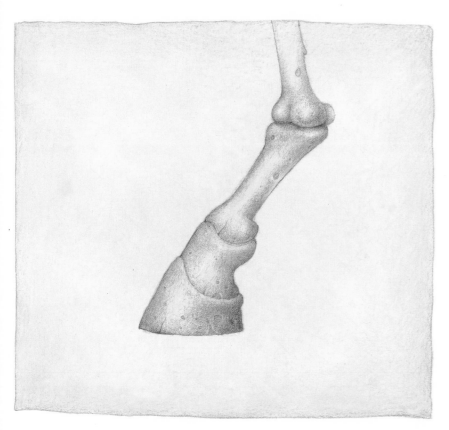

suffocating her to death. However, the Jade Emperor of Heaven had been following this drama with interest, and stepped in to save the girl. He changed her into a cocoon and when she emerged from it like a silk-moth he carried her up to heaven to become his lover.

Like certain statues of Demeter in Greece, Lady Horse-head is sometimes portrayed as literally having a horse's head, but more often she is shown as a beautiful maid. She is the guardian of silkworms, but the inventor of silk-making was Xi Ling, the wife of the great Yellow Emperor, Huang Di. One day, as she was drinking tea under a mulberry tree in the palace gardens, a moth cocoon fell into her cup. In the hot tea it unravelled and the Empress immediately saw what fine thread it made.

Finally, when considering the horse, the Chinese might think of those that draw the chariot of the sun. This is driven by the god (or sometimes goddess) of the sun, Xi Ho, who rises at dawn from the fabled Islands of the Immortals in the Region of Sweet Waters in the south-eastern ocean. Cousins of these flying steeds often appear in legend as the famous *Thousand Li* horses that could cover over 300 miles (500km) in a day.

Besides this sun chariot, the whole world is often shown in Chinese scrolls as a square chariot whose round canopy forms the sky.

The Princess of Chin
raises her blinds
Dawn at the northern
window
She points to Xi Ho
in the east
Deftly urging his steeds
While land begins to rise
from the sea
And stone hills wear away.

Li He (790–816)

The Horse in Legend and Lore

A tale that was ancient even at the time it was written down during the Han dynasty (c. 200 BC to AD 220) tells of a king threatened by the Huns who wanted a Thousand Li horse to patrol his borders. He offered a bag of gold as reward to anyone who could find him one. A visiting sage assured him that it would be no trouble and off he went. A week later he returned with a sack of bones that he laid before the king.

'Here you are,' he told the king. 'Here is a very famous flying horse. Admittedly it has been dead awhile, but for that reason I will only accept half your reward.'

'What use to me is a dead flying horse?' cried the king, almost beside himself with rage and signalling his executioner.

'Well, look at it this way,' replied the sage, 'when the news spreads that you're ready to pay so much for a dead flying horse, think how likely someone is to bring you a living one!'

The king calmed down, thought about it, and finally paid the sage half a bag of gold. Within a year he was the proud owner of three living Thousand Li horses that proved well worth the gold he paid for them.

Despite their great love of horses and the extravagant lengths many emperors went to in building up their herds, the Chinese have always considered their own horses inferior to those of the 'barbarian nomads' of Central Asia. At times most of their silk exports simply paid for fresh bloodstocks imported from Mongolia and sometimes as far away as Arabia.

During the Han dynasty the most prized horses in China, for both hardiness and intelligence, were those of their great enemies, the Huns, who were first united as a kind of mobile empire under the great King Mao-tun, who killed his father for the crown. When one of the subject tribes objected to this crime, Mao-tun pacified them with a gift of his father's own steed, one of the legendary Thousand Li horses.

For hundreds of years, when the Huns could not simply take things by force, they traded their horses with the Chinese for silk, wine and grain. In times of weakness, the Empire often bought peace with lavish bribes or tried to forge alliances by marriage, until finally they were strong enough to defy the nomad hordes. The Huns then grew restless and went west to plunder Europe instead. A favourite musical instrument among their descendants in Mongolia and northern China today is the horse-head violin or *Morin Khuur*, a two-stringed instrument played with a bow. Legend says that it was invented by a man who was so grief-stricken by the death of his horse that he made a violin from its bones.

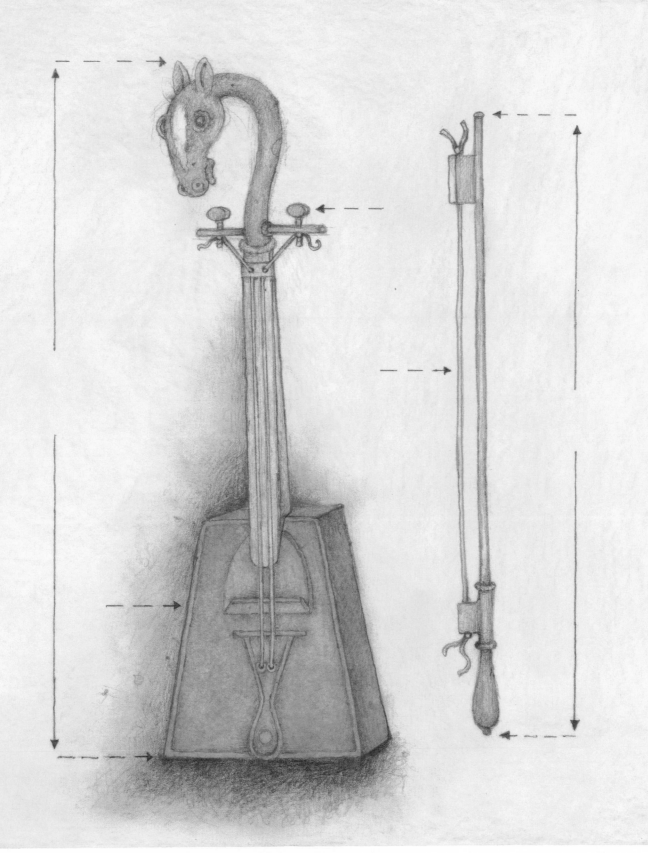

During the great Tang dynasty (seventh to ninth centuries AD), one of the high periods of Chinese culture, it is on record that fifty million feet of silk were traded with the nomads one year for horses, and this was a good time for China's horse stock. The Six Steeds of Emperor Tai Zong, who forged the dynasty (although he courteously allowed his father to reign before him), are the most famous in Chinese history. These are the six horses he rode into the many battles by which he unified the Empire, some of which were killed beneath him. They came from Persia and were immortalized in stone at Tai Zong's magnificent tomb on Mount Jiuzong, near Xi'an city in the Shaanxi Province. Stories are still told today celebrating each one's exploits and manner of death.

Besides these favourites, Tai Zong kept some 40,000 other horses in his stables and introduced the game of polo from Persia to hone the riding skills of his cavalry. This emperor's tomb complex was as rambling as any palace for the living, but as an inscription there says: 'A ruler takes the whole world under heaven as his realm, why then should he keep treasures inside his tomb, possessing them as his private property? Now that my tomb has been built on Jiuzong Shan with no gold, no jade, no slaves nor horses within, and household utensils made of clay and wood, thieves and robbers will cease their attempts, saving trouble for everyone.'

EMPEROR TAI ZONG

The flavour of these mild times is that there are no heroes.
I love the lone cloud's idleness and the stillness of the monks.
Before I'm gone, banner in hand, to the river and the sea
From the plain above the capital I'll look out on Tai Zong's tomb.

BOOK OF TANG, NINTH CENTURY AD

Year of the Horse

Horses were China's main defence against the Western hordes, but often they conquered China anyway and then settled there to found new dynasties, as with the Yuan dynasty founded by Genghis Khan in 1260. These Tartars, Huns or Mongols added their own love of horses to the native Chinese tradition as they were gradually absorbed into the culture. It is said that Genghis's followers could ride for weeks without supplies, drinking only their horses' milk and blood. This was why they were so deadly. They were almost one with their beasts and possibly gave rise to the Greek myth of centaurs.

The war-chariots rattle,
The war-horses neigh:
Each man of you has a bow and quiver at his belt.
Father, mother, wife and son watch your leaving
Till dust buries the bridge beyond Ch'ang-an.

PING CH'E HSING, TANG DYNASTY

KUBLAI KHAN

Generations later, Marco Polo in his *Travels* describes how Genghis's grandson, Kublai Khan, ruler of the largest empire the world had ever seen, stretching from the China Sea to the Levant, kept a herd of 20,000 snow-white horses, stallions and mares. These were picked from the 100,000 or so presented to him each New Year by his subjects. The milk from this herd could not be drunk by anyone outside the royal family, save for members of a certain tribe who had been granted this favour long before by Genghis Khan as a battle honour. These spotless horses were so honoured that even the highest-ranking travellers would detour around the herd, or wait patiently for it to pass of its own accord before proceeding on their way. For three months every summer Kublai Khan would erect his pleasure dome at Shang-tu, beyond the Great Wall, where he kept these fabulous beasts. Then, on a day appointed by his astrologers, he would leave to make a sacrifice of their milk to certain spirits so they would 'guard all his possessions, men and women, birds, beasts, crops and everything else besides'.

The Horse in Legend and Lore

A Fable

Near the northern border lived a man whose horse
ran off one day into the country of
the nomads. His neighbours all said how sorry they were,
but the man only shrugged philosophically and said,
'Maybe it will turn out a blessing.'

Everyone marvelled at his optimism, but then a few months later the horse
did return, bringing as a companion the finest mare anyone had ever seen.
Now they marvelled at the man's good luck, but he only said thoughtfully,
'Perhaps no good will come of it.'

Soon afterwards, his son fell off the mare and broke his leg.
The neighbours again commiserated, but the man just said,
'Who knows, perhaps some good will come of this.'

Not long after, barbarians poured over the border and every
able-bodied man was sent off to war. Nine out of ten from that
district died before peace was restored. Those of his
neighbours who had survived watched the man and
his son going contentedly about their lives
and this time said nothing at all.

Chapter Two

The Astrological Sign of the Horse

IN CHINESE ASTROLOGY THE SIGN OF THE HORSE

HAS ABSORBED INTO ITSELF ALL THE ASSOCIATIONS MENTIONED IN THE LAST CHAPTER,

PLUS COUNTLESS OTHERS ABOUT WHICH WE CAN ONLY SURMISE.

THESE HAVE ALL ADDED UP TO WHAT ASTROLOGERS DEFINE AS THE CHARACTER OF THE HORSE.

One must remember, though, that unless you were born in the hour and month of the Horse as well as the year, this profile is not intended to be a close portrait. It is a description of the ideal pattern or template of the Horse personality – the Platonic idea, if you will. It is an influence or tendency, a complex of linked character traits that affect the individual, but only to the degree that it is present in their chart. If a person's year sign is the Horse with the month sign of the Rat, for example, the two signs will pull in opposite directions because they are about as different as can be. How individuals resolve such tensions is what defines their unique personality.

General Character Traits of the Horse

GIVE AN OLD HORSE ITS HEAD WHEN YOU ARE LOST, AND IT WILL LEAD YOU HOME.

CONFUCIUS, *SPRING AND AUTUMN ANNALS* 22

In China, the horse is a symbol of nobility, elegance, speed, perseverance, strength and courage; but it is worth remembering Confucius's dictum: 'A good horse is not praised for its strength, but for its character' (*Analects* 14:35). This is a reminder that all these virtues are worthless if not channelled correctly. Courage can easily become arrogance or high-handedness. Speed and strength can as easily be employed for evil as for good. So the Horse (along with the Dragon and the Tiger, which also stand for nobility) has to pay special heed to the ancient Chinese precepts for noble behaviour laid down by Confucius, Lao Tzu and other sages.

The natural Horse temperament is optimistic, generous, loyal, honest and sociable. The Horse also loves to travel, either physically or in the sense of constantly moving on from one project to another. This restlessness can cause problems, but luckily Horses are also gifted with great practical sense. They have a talent for making their ideas work before moving on and a charm that makes them welcome wherever they go.

Regarding marriage, the Horse's gregariousness and yearning for new horizons often do raise problems, but Horses are rarely single for long. They have a magnetic attraction for the opposite sex, a glamour that often seduces more cautious partners even when their better judgement tells them the liaison cannot last. However, the Horse's sense of adventure is contagious, and their natural honesty and openness makes them easier to forgive than most people after romantic misadventures.

Horses thrive best in situations where they are free to use their own initiative. Capable of intense loyalty to their superiors, they expect it to be repaid with trust in making their own judgements. Horses also like company and to be at the centre of a crowd. They make great diplomats, travelling merchants and military officers, occupations that constantly throw up new faces and challenges.

On the negative side, restlessness can in some cases lead to the Horse becoming arrogant and insensitive to others' needs, although arrogance is not a commonplace problem with Horses because they are mostly far too good-natured. The Horses' self-reliance is often the key to their success in life, but it can be taken too far. Horses are generally less independent than they seem. They enjoy having an audience to witness and applaud their victories.

Adventurousness may lead the Horse to rush into situations without realizing all the complications, but they are usually equal to tackling the problems that arise. Their charm and enthusiasm often gets new ventures going where greater caution fails. Horses are great motivators, even though others may be left to cope with the finer details.

The most compatible signs for the Horse are the Dog or the Tiger. The most incompatible is the Rat.

Elements

The animal signs of Chinese astrology are often called the Twelve Earthly Branches because they are believed to be the channels by which the Divine manifests itself on the earthly plane. The five elements in their Yin and Yang polarities are often known as the Ten Heavenly Stems because they are the links between the signs and their source. Only half the stems get applied to each sign however, because it is always either Yin or Yang. The Horse, for instance, is always Yang; it is just the element that changes each time.

We do not need to know much about the elements for our purposes here, beyond showing how they influence the fundamental Horse personality, but it is interesting to compare them for a moment with the four elements of Western philosophy. At first the Chinese choice of five seems odd, until one realizes that the fifth element belongs to the centre. This is exactly equivalent to the Quintessence or Fifth Element of the West, the only real difference being that the Chinese talk about it more.

A simple way of remembering the Chinese elements is to picture a cauldron of water heating over an open fire. Approaching it from above, the first thing you touch is the metal of the cauldron's handles. Then you meet the water within it, then the ends of the wood sticking up out of the flames around the cauldron, then the fire itself and finally the earth below that.

One of the novelties of visiting China was coming across occasional reversals in things we take so much for granted. Having developed largely in isolation from the West, China has addressed the same dilemmas and often come up with quite opposing answers, such as choosing to wear white at funerals, and reading from right to left. Maps are another instance. We always have north at the top but in China it is usually the reverse. For this chart however, although it is based on a Chinese original, we have indulged the sensitivities of our readers by placing north in its familiar place at the top.

This is also the order in which the elements rotate through the Chinese calendar, occupying two years at a time, the first having a Yang polarity and the second a Yin. So a Yang Metal year is followed by a Yin Metal year; then a Yang Water year is followed by a Yin Water year and so on.

The element of your birth year can be told very simply by taking the last digit and putting it into the table below.

0	Metal-Yang	Keng
1	Metal-Yin	Hsin
2	Water-Yang	Jen
3	Water-Yin	Kuei
4	Wood-Yang	Chia
5	Wood-Yin	Yi
6	Fire-Yang	Ping
7	Fire-Yin	Ting
8	Earth-Yang	Mou
9	Earth-Yin	Chi

So now you know the element of your year sign, read on to see how it affects the Horse.

The Astrological Sign of the Horse

Metal Horse

30 January 1930 to 17 February 1931 / 27 January 1990 to 15 February 1991

THE ELEMENT METAL
POSITIVE QUALITIES: strength, wealth, success, perseverance, virtue
NEGATIVE QUALITIES: stubbornness, inflexibility
ASSOCIATED PLANET: VENUS

Effect on the Horse: The element Metal gives this Horse greater perseverance than others. He or she waits until a project is up and running before scanning the horizon for fresh challenges. Confident and charismatic, Metal Horses generally succeed at whatever they set their minds to. They stand out from the crowd. Though occasionally impulsive or stubborn, the Metal Horse's natural humour quickly soothes any ruffled feelings caused by this.

Water Horse

15 February 1942 to 5 February 1943 / 12 February 2002 to 1 February 2003

THE ELEMENT WATER
POSITIVE QUALITIES: creativeness, adaptability, empathy with others, fluency and communicativeness
NEGATIVE QUALITIES: inconsistency
ASSOCIATED PLANET: MERCURY

Effect on the Horse: Water tends to bring out the charm in Horses, but also enhances their restlessness. Water Horses make great adventurers and entertainers with leanings towards music and the arts, but often have difficult domestic lives. They are better suited to the stage than the civil service or marriage. Because of their restless curiosity, they are usually great conversationalists and most of their anecdotes will come from personal experience.

The Astrological Sign of the Horse

ROCKING HORSES FOR CHILDREN ARE MENTIONED IN SOME VERY ANCIENT TALES AND WOULD SEEM TO HAVE BEEN FIRST INVENTED IN CHINA.

Wood Horse

3 February 1954 to 24 January 1955

THE ELEMENT WOOD
POSITIVE QUALITIES: supportiveness, generosity, strength, self-sacrifice
NEGATIVE QUALITIES: not knowing own limits
ASSOCIATED PLANET: JUPITER

Effect on the Horse: The Wood Horse is naturally one of the happiest and most easy-going of the signs.
Brave, cheerful, friendly, trustworthy and ever-willing to lend a helping hand,
the main problem Wood Horses have is being too trusting of others.
A good friend and loyal partner, their happiness often depends on those around them keeping a watch on their blind side.

Year of the Horse

Fire Horse

21 January 1966 to 9 February 1967

THE ELEMENT FIRE
POSITIVE QUALITIES: passion, action, determination, perceptiveness
NEGATIVE QUALITIES: impulsiveness
ASSOCIATED PLANET: MARS

Effect on the Horse: Because Fire is the Horse's natural element, being born in a Fire year will tempt a person to extremes. They tend either to succeed or fail spectacularly. Much depends on luck in finding situations where their extreme energies are appreciated; or on finding a partner able to temper their excesses. In China, many women try to avoid giving birth in Fire Horse years because of the turmoil that is sure to follow. Fire Horses often achieve renown and are widely loved and admired, but they can be hard work for their immediate friends and family. They don't take kindly to outside interference in their affairs and can often be brusque.

The Astrological Sign of the Horse

Earth Horse

11 February 1918 to 1 February 1919 / 7 February 1978 to 28 January 1979

THE ELEMENT EARTH

POSITIVE QUALITIES: patience, attention to detail, reliability, common sense, sympathy
NEGATIVE QUALITIES: self-absorption
ASSOCIATED PLANET: SATURN

Effect on the Horse: The Earth Horse has a deceptively quiet and conventional outer manner (for a Horse)
that hides a fascination with new and often revolutionary ideas. This is the Horse whose restlessness is concentrated in the world of ideas
and, unlike the extremist, is gifted at both making them work and selling them to others.
Far more modest than, say, the Fire Horse, the Earth Horse will often let others take the credit just as long as a thing gets done.

WAR OFTEN BRINGS OUT THE BEST QUALITIES OF THE HORSE; SUCH AS COURAGE, INITIATIVE, LEADERSHIP AND A WILLINGNESS TO RISK THEIR LIVES FOR OTHERS. MOST HORSES READILY ADAPT TO THE GENTLER ADVENTURES OF PEACETIME, BUT THE FIRE HORSE OFTEN SEEMS ONLY FULLY AT HOME AMID THE TURMOIL AND CHAOS OF THE BATTLEFIELD.

Chapter Three

Friends and Enemies

By now you should be familiar with your Chinese astrological profile. Assuming your year sign is the Horse, you will in addition have an element for the year, which gives a slant to your birth sign. This will be, according to the Chinese astrologer, the tendency with which you face the world. If you are a Fire Horse, say, you may well often find yourself tempted to start conflicts to achieve your ends; whereas a Water or Wood Horse, given the same set of ambitions, will tend to achieve them with far less noise and commotion.

You will also be familiar with your month and possibly your hour signs, and a glance at the chart opposite should immediately show how comfortably they sit with that of the year. A simple guide is that opposite signs clash while those that are linked by triangles are most in harmony.

If your month sign also happens to be the Horse, then the chances are that you are one of those happy souls that are rarely at odds with themselves. Also, you are likely to have recognized yourself clearly in the last chapter. But don't get too complacent, double-signed people may rarely suffer from self-doubt but this can often make them hard to bear. They are so sure of themselves that they find it hard to see other people's viewpoints, and this often drives them away. In China, great generals are

often said to have been born with a double Horse sign. This makes them good and popular leaders, but they suffer from the loneliness of high office.

Conversely, if your month sign is opposite your year sign in the circle, it is in the least comfortable position. Horses whose month sign is the Rat will often feel themselves pulled in opposite directions because their inner inclinations will be at odds with how they feel they are expected to behave. This can, however, become a virtue. While you may at times envy the blithe self-confidence of others, an inner tension like this can produce a creative fire that is more effective than pure self-confidence. You are more likely to listen to others and achieve by diplomacy what the double Horse gains by leading from the front. It takes greater patience, self-consciousness and wisdom to succeed as a Rat Horse, but the success is likely to last longer. Just as the double Horse needs to guard against complacency, the Rat Horse must guard against being too self-critical.

For those born in a year of the Horse, the two most harmonious month signs after the Horse itself are the Dog and the Tiger. These are equally spaced around the circle from the Horse and are its natural friends and allies. Astrologers say that the sign on the left, the Dog in this case, is the helpful friend, the undemanding minister or partner who enjoys supporting your projects without asking for much in return. The Tiger, on the right, is more of an ally than a friend, someone who will share your cause but not necessarily become close. The advantage for a Horse of having either the Dog or the Tiger in their month of birth is that there is a natural harmony, plus emotional breadth. Such people suffer from neither the occasionally overweening confidence of the

double Horse, nor the self-destructive doubts of the Rat Horse.

The other signs fall between these four extremes much as the points of a compass do between north, south, east and west. So the Boar and the Ox could be good allies, but will require more effort than, say, the Rooster or the Hare.

The same procedure can be followed with your hour sign. Mark it on the chart on page 49 and see how well it relates to your month and year signs. If it is in opposition to either, this might explain why your reactions to certain situations are not what you expect. Unless your goals and achievements satisfy your most secret self as well as your more conscious one, you can never expect to feel fully satisfied with anything you do. Consequently, if your inner sign is in opposition to the others, you would be wise to study it because it is the key to feeling fulfilled.

The chart can also be useful for gauging how well you will relate to other people. For instance, if your year signs are in opposition you can expect to have constant differences of opinion about what life is all about. As with all differences, this is not necessarily a bad thing because the most creative relationships are between opposites, but it will cause arguments. If your year signs are in opposition but your month sign is in harmony with any aspect of the other person's profile, then the dialogue will be eased. If all aspects of your chart clash with all aspects of theirs, well, life is just too short for some challenges and it may just be simplest to avoid the person. But bear in mind that all Chinese philosophy is based on the principle that reconciling opposites is always better than going to war over them.

Review of the Signs

RAT *Shu*

AMBITIOUS, PRACTICAL, CHARMING, QUICK-WITTED

Legend says that the order of the beasts in the Chinese zodiac was decided by the order in which they answered the Buddha's summons. The rat beat the patient, sturdy ox into first place by secretly riding on its back and then jumping off at the finishing line. Many Westerners find it off-putting to learn that their sign is the Rat, so deep is their loathing and fear of the creature, but the Chinese accord it much respect, in the abstract at least. So to them it is no insult at all to have the Rat as their birth sign.

Partly, the rat is admired for its cleverness, as demonstrated by the legend. Another tale speaks of how, during the great period of chaos before the world was properly formed, the rat bit Confusion and drove it away, allowing the sky and earth to separate, as we know them today. Also, rats are associated with wealth because by choice they seek the rich man's barn, so a rat's blessing is said to bring wealth and happiness. In the Fukien Province in the south they say it was the rat who gave the first rice seeds to humankind, so we owe it a portion of the harvest in return. The Chinese often even encourage rats into their barns in the hope that they will bring prosperity with them. In Peking, the third day of the New Year is said to be when the Rat's daughter gets married, but the date varies around New Year in different parts of the Empire. Many people go to bed early that night so as not to disturb the rats' nuptials. Seeds are sprinkled in the corners of house and barn for the wedding feast and in the hope that this will be repaid with the blessing of a good harvest.

When rats are heard scrabbling in the shadows they are said to be counting their money, but 'Money Rat' is a term of abuse for misers.

People born under the sign of the Rat are generally optimistic, intelligent, sociable and dependable. They are imaginative and very adaptable to new circumstances. Ambitious, practical, charming and quick-witted, the danger for the Rat is of getting carried away with its own cleverness and going too far. The Horse will be the first to spot this as, being natural enemies, they each tend to see only each other's faults. The Rat, to its enemy, seems scheming, devious and underhand, while the Horse seems vain, loud-mouthed and dressy. It takes great diplomacy for a Horse and a Rat to become friends.

OX *Niu*

PATIENT, RELIABLE, DETERMINED, INTELLIGENT, STRONG, PERSEVERING

The fifth day of the New Year celebrations is celebrated in Peking as the birthday of the Ox; the farmer's patient draught animal since ancient times. Farmers' wealth is measured in terms of how many oxen or cows they have and so they care for their beasts well. The spring festival of the Ox marks the start of the agricultural year, when many oracles are consulted about the prospects of a good harvest.

The seventh day of the seventh month is dedicated to a cowherd who, in ancient times, fell in love with the goddess Weaving Maid. With the aid of the Immortal Ox of Heaven, he succeeded in winning her heart but their love offended Xi Wang Mu, the Queen of Heaven. The Ox showed the cowherd the secret of immortality but still Xi Wang Mu would not be swayed and drew the Milky Way with her hairpin to separate them. However the King of Heaven, the Jade Emperor, took pity and allowed them to meet one day a year, on the seventh day of the seventh moon of the year.

The Ox was originally a star deity that lived only in heaven. Considering how hard humans had to work in tilling the earth, the Jade Emperor one day sent the Ox star down to teach them how, if they worked diligently, they would be able to eat happily every third day. But the Ox mixed up the message, promising them they would feed three times a day if they only followed the instructions. As punishment, his return was barred and he was obliged to help fulfil his rash promise by helping humans plough their fields. This legend is commemorated by the star many oxen still have on their brows.

The Ox is a symbol of peace because in peacetime it is mostly seen ploughing the fields to produce an abundant harvest for its masters. In gratitude for its faithful labour many Chinese will not eat beef, and some emperors have even made this a crime.

People born under the sign of the Ox are dependable, patient and hard working, often achieving success late in life when others are abandoning ambition for thoughts of retirement. Their quiet perseverance often succeeds where more volatile characters like the Dragon and the Tiger fail.

The Ox and the Horse do not have many tastes in common because it is often the Ox who has to finish what the Horse begins, carrying projects through to completion long after their originator has forgotten all about them. However, both are hard workers by any other standards and, as with the Pig, can often work together harmoniously in the right conditions. They even enjoy each other's company, but usually only for the time they are engaged on some joint undertaking. Marriage between Oxen and Horses tends to be problematical.

Friends & Enemies

TIGER *Hu*

PASSIONATE, AMBITIOUS, BRAVE, CONFIDENT, IMPULSIVE

The Tiger is the king of animals in its strength and courage. In places it is feared so much that people will not even whisper its name, but will refer to it instead as the King of the Mountains or, more obscurely, *da chong* meaning 'large insect'. When a district is troubled by tigers generally the people will not try to kill them but rather make offerings and politely ask them to move away, which it seems they often do.

The White Tiger also represents the west and autumn, as the Black Tortoise does the north and winter, the Green Dragon the east and spring and the Red Phoenix the south and summer. So the Tiger is patron of the annual harvest and is often shown bearing the god of the district on its back. It is also the Lord of Death.

Legend holds that the Tiger was born from a star that fell from the constellation of the Plough and it is a lord of the winds.

Because of its fearless strength, the Chinese often have representations of the Tiger guarding their homes and tombs against robbers and demons. Tiger-skin cloaks or saddle-cloths are highly prized for the same reason by nobles and generals, while the less wealthy weave the pattern into their cloaks.

People born under the sign of the Tiger are brave, strong and outgoing. They protect the weak against those who are stronger and are never happier than when righting some real or imagined wrong.

The Tiger and the Horse are natural allies, though the Horse often has to rein in its natural assertiveness and let the Tiger feel in charge. If this is feasible, then their alliance will prosper for both parties. Years of the Tiger tend to be very prosperous for the Horse, though often a bit too exciting for comfort.

HARE *Tu*

SOCIABLE, GENEROUS, INTUITIVE, MODEST

In the Warring States period (c. 500–220 BC) the Prime Minister of the Qi state, Meng Changjun sent a servant to collect the rent from his tenant farmers. The servant, Feng Xuan, found the farmers suffering from poor crops and so boldly told them they were excused their rent. When his master heard of this he was furious, but Feng Xuan said: 'The wily hare has three burrows to escape the fox. Likewise, you may have lost the rent but you have gained the love of your tenants and, who knows, one day that may be worth more to you than gold.'

The wisdom of these words was proved a year or so later when Meng Changjun was dismissed from office and sent home, where his grateful peasants greeted him with joy. So he thanked his servant for his far-sightedness. Feng Xuan, however, said: 'The wily hare has three burrows but you now have only one. If you want my advice, what you should now do is visit the state of Wei (which was at war with Qi) and tell them a little of what you did as Prime Minister of Qi. But when they offer you a position, as they surely will, you must refuse. This will get the attention of the King of Qi, and then we'll see what happens.'

Meng Changjun followed this advice and, true enough, when the King of Qi heard that his enemies were trying to tempt Meng into their service, he immediately restored him as Prime Minister. He also offered many other rich gifts but, on his servant's advice, Meng Changjun refused them all, asking only that he be allowed to build a new temple near his home, both for the spiritual welfare of his tenants and as a refuge should war come that way. This request was granted and when the work was done Feng Xuan said to his master: 'Now you have your three burrows: the love of your king, the love of your people and a place to shelter should all else fail. You can rest easy.' And so it proved, for Meng remained Prime Minister to the end of his long and happy life.

once, when the Buddha was starving, all the forest creatures brought him what food they could. The rabbit had nothing to offer so it leaped on to the fire and gave itself. In gratitude, the Buddha set the rabbit's face on the shining face of the moon where it can still be seen today. It is commonly believed, even where hares are common and people should know better, that they are all female and become pregnant by eating the shoots of certain plants.

People born under the sign of the Rabbit are mild, generous and peace-loving. They are adaptable and sensitive, sociable and popular. They are also perfectionists in their work and often make good artists and craftsmen.

In Indo-China, the totem animal for this month is the Cat, but despite their very different natures in reality, the characteristics of the signs are much the same; the cats being viewed from a human viewpoint rather than, say, that of a mouse or songbird. This is the graceful house cat that has charmed and beguiled humans since the earliest times when it sauntered into our lives and curled up by the fire.

The Hare or Rabbit (both terms are used for this sign) is one of the friendliest and gentlest of the signs. Although timid by nature, it is also nimble, sensitive, and proverbially clever.

The Hare is a symbol of long life because the Goddess of the Moon, Chang O, lives there with a hare that spends its time pounding the roots of the sacred Cassia [Cinnamon] tree with a pestle and mortar to make an elixir of immortality. At the Mid-autumn Festival people pray to the Goddess for some of this to prolong their lives.

The hare or rabbit is also said to thrive during periods of sound government, so to attract good fortune the Empress Wu of the Tang dynasty built a Temple of the Rabbit. Legend says that

The Hare and the Horse make good friends, the gentle, modest Hare tempering the Horse's natural inclination to prance about and show off. In the Hare's company the Horse can relax and enjoy the simple pleasures of life for a while. Often they make good marriage partners, but the astrologers say this depends very much on other aspects of their chart also being in harmony.

Friends & Enemies

DRAGON *Long*

MAGNIFICENT, INSPIRING, DECISIVE, BOLD, IMAGINATIVE

The dragon is the most pervasive image in Chinese art and iconography and is, more than any other creature, the symbol of the Chinese spirit, emblematic of the Emperor and Heaven. It is the only purely fanciful creature in the zodiac, but to most Chinese it is not fanciful at all. For evidence, they will show the dragons' bones on sale in every market, which for centuries have been mined from the earth in certain regions where they are plentiful. The earliest emperors are said to have been part dragon and to have had supernatural powers, especially over the weather.

To this day, many Chinese unquestioningly believe that it is dragons who control the rain on which their crops and livelihoods depend, who can as easily unleash drought or flood. They are rarely held vindictive in this, though. Most dragons are highly revered and calamitous weather is blamed more on oversight than any desire to harm people. To remind dragons of our existence, the Chinese take care to observe the feasts devoted to dragons, especially to remind them when it is time to leave their underwater winter palaces and take to the skies to make rain. There are countless temples by lakes and rivers where offerings are made. In ancient times these included human sacrifices. The most beautiful maidens were cast into lakes weighed down with stones to become brides for the dragon lords, and it was believed they lived long and happy lives underwater, for their husbands could take human form and their palaces were filled with jewels and splendour. Later, the offerings were of jade, gems and delicate foodstuffs.

Years of the Dragon are held to be lucky for everyone, but especially those who have it as their year, month or hour sign.

The Horse prospers as much as any sign in years of the Dragon, having a natural fondness for the pomp, glamour and flamboyance that are the Dragon's forte. They make a good team in business and war, and often make spectacular, if tempestuous, marriages.

SNAKE *She*

MYSTERIOUS, INTELLIGENT, DISCIPLINED, TASTEFUL

As in other parts of the world, in China the snake is regarded with equal fascination and fear. Being a relation of the dragon, it abounds in ancient legend, often approaching the status of a god, but it is also a common and dangerous creature that might be met any day. It is listed as one of the Five Noxious Creatures along with the centipede, scorpion, gecko and toad, but equally, many snakes are used in medicine, especially their livers. Some are highly prized as culinary delights and their flesh is said to be good for the eyesight, but the fat is believed poisonous.

The guardian spirit of the north, the Dark Warrior Xuan Wu, is often represented as a snake entwined with a turtle. In some parts of the country it is still commonly believed that the two can mate in real life to produce strange offspring, though in the cities this is dismissed as quaint rural superstition.

The Snake is a Yin creature closely associated with the female. If a pregnant woman dreams of a black snake it is a sure sign she will give birth to a girl. The Snake is sometimes associated with wiliness and treachery. There is a popular legend about a white snake that was able to take the appearance of a beautiful woman and seduce young men to her dinner table. But the Snake is better known for repaying kindness with treasure, near which it likes to make its nest. Keeping a snakeskin in the house is believed a sure way of attracting wealth.

Because it regularly sheds its skin, the snake is a symbol of longevity through rebirth. Dreams of being wrapped in a snake's coils usually mean some big change in life is about to happen.

In astrology, the Snake is considered clever but having a tendency towards manipulation and deviousness that needs to be kept under control.

The Horse and the Snake have the attraction of opposites. Their basic approaches to life are almost as different as possible but they rarely clash. The subtle Snake and unassuming Horse often comically misunderstand each other, so different is their mode of thinking, and often the Horse will fall totally under the spell of the mysterious Snake for a while, before robust common sense returns.

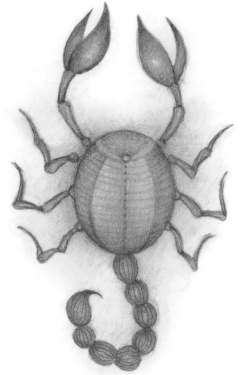

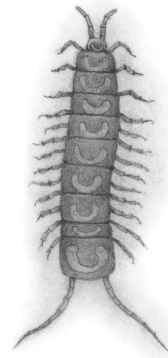

Friends & Enemies

HORSE *Ma*

ADVENTUROUS, BRAVE, SOCIABLE, INTELLIGENT

See its own chapter for discussion of the Horse temperament, but what one can say here is that in its own years the Horse, like the other signs, can act out its own nature more freely than usual. This is a good time for facing up to challenges that threaten your chosen way of life, but it is best to let them come to you rather than going out to seek them. One must beware of reckless adventures, especially in Fire Horse years, which are often times of war and revolution. The dangers to which the Horse is naturally attracted are real enough, so apart from courage, this is also a time for testing the practical sense for which the Horse is renowned. It is a time for proving one's worth, but the chances are you will only be able to relax and reap the benefits the following year, that of the Goat.

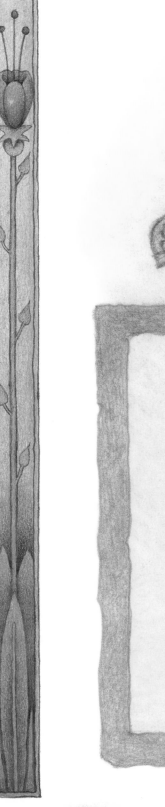

GOAT *Yang*

IMAGINATIVE, CHARMING, ADAPTABLE, LOYAL

The Goat (or Sheep, there seems no clear distinction in Chinese) is associated with good fortune and prosperity, because it is in such times that it thrives. The Goat is graceful and charming, but imaginative, too and often finds expression through the fine arts. The Goat appreciates order and beauty, peace and calm. The excitements it best enjoys are of an aesthetic or philosophical nature. The Goat, in fact, has much in common with the Hare, but with fewer supernatural overtones.

The Goat is renowned for its courage when forced to defend what it holds dear, also its loyalty, especially towards parents. A kid down on its knees and seemingly praying in order to suckle from its mother is often employed as a symbol of filial piety.

The Goat is naturally the best of friends with the Horse, to whom it looks for protection in times of trouble. When Horses return from the battlefront they are sure of a warm welcome and an appreciative audience for their tales. Their achievements will be recognized and rewarded. Where the Horse is the guardian of peace, the Goat is the guardian of the arts that flourish in peacetime and give life its savour. They generally recognize and enjoy their interdependence, so in whatever field it applies, this is a lucky combination.

Friends & Enemies

MONKEY *Hou*

ENTERTAINING, WITTY, IMAGINATIVE, ADAPTABLE

The Monkey god is a hero of the Ming dynasty tale *Journey to the West* and his antics are as familiar to Chinese children as *Jack and the Beanstalk* is to ours. In this tale, Monkey is set to guard the Peach Trees of Immortality in the garden of the Queen Mother of the West, Xi Wang Mu. These bear fruit only once every 6,000 years, when the Queen Mother holds a great feast on her birthday, at which the precious peaches are shared out among the Immortals, for it is the peaches that grant everlasting life.

However, on the eve of the banquet Monkey ate the lot. For punishment, the Jade Emperor of Heaven handed him over to the Buddha, who despatched him off to India with the Buddhist monk Xuan-cang to bring back original copies of the Buddhist scriptures, because those in China were corrupt. After many adventures which tested his courage, wit and ingenuity to the limit, Monkey returned with both the scriptures and great wisdom, and has been revered as a god ever since, though he has not completely lost his fondness for mischief and practical jokes.

Apart from anything else, this tale shows how comfortably the three main religions of China – Confucianism, Taoism and Buddhism – sit alongside each other. This tolerance can seem curious to the Western mind because the Buddha and Jade Emperor technically belong to different cosmologies. One reason for the easy acceptance of Buddhism in China around the time of our Lord is that many Chinese believe that the Buddha was in fact Lao Tzu, the founder of Taoism, who disappeared into the West after writing his famous book the *Tao Te Ching*. Perhaps this co-existence of religious traditions explains their ready acceptance of Christian missionaries. The danger we find is that one is lulled into the same easy tolerance of other beliefs, which can come as a shock to friends and colleagues fresh from home.

In astrology the Monkey personality is bright, witty, entertaining and popular. The Monkey has a nimble mind and can turn a hand to almost any occupation that comes along. He is also eager to help others with his many talents and will delight as much in praise as monetary reward. The downfall of the Monkey is often his irrepressible curiosity and sometimes misplaced sense of fun. Usually he shines best when in the service of another, when his sense of loyalty will override his instinct for mischief. Female Monkeys tend to be more stable than the males and often in them it is only the virtues of the sign that show.

The Horse and the Monkey chime quite well, as long as the Monkey does not try to take command. Often the Horse finds the Monkey too light-hearted and capricious for long-term partnership, but they tend on the whole to be good for each other, being well aware of each other's weaknesses. Years of the Monkey tend to be full of surprises for Horses, often unwelcome ones that test their humour to the limit, but rarely anything seriously unpleasant.

Friends & Enemies

ROOSTER *Ji*

FLAMBOYANT, BRAVE, PROTECTIVE, RELIABLE

The Rooster or Cockerel is credited with the five virtues of literacy, strength, courage, benevolence and loyalty, and in all the parts of China that we have visited, we never once heard of a rooster being eaten, though of course his wives are less fortunate. The Rooster is considered a scholar because his comb looks much like the scholars' hats of old. His strength lies in his spurs and his courage is demonstrated by his eagerness to fight to the death over his territory. The Rooster is generous and always calls his wives to food when he finds it, and loyal because he never fails to wake the farm at dawn. He is also believed to guard the home at night against fire and demons. The image of a white rooster is often placed in tombs to guard the dead. At one time, a real rooster would be sacrificed and buried with its owner, and apparently this still happens, but most Chinese are now content to take a carving or image on a piece of paper into the afterlife.

In astrology, the Rooster bears all these qualities and in addition is said to be a good administrator with a meticulous eye for detail. Occasionally he suffers from being arrogant, overbearing and pompous, but is soon forgiven because of his finer qualities. Curiously, ladies in China who have the Rooster as their sign seem not to be expected to be 'hens'; that is, to be passive, not very clever and destined for the pot when they stop laying eggs. Female Roosters are instead credited with all the talents of the male, though they are expected to display them in a more genteel and restrained manner.

The Rooster and the Horse are not exactly enemies but neither do they find it easy to get along. Both like pomp and display, both are ready to fight to the death for their ideals, but the Rooster cannot understand the Horse's yearning for new horizons. Once he has his territory, that is enough. Years of the Rooster tend to feel oppressive to Horses and the best they can do is be patient and wait for them to pass.

DOG *Gou*

LOYAL, SOCIABLE, BRAVE,
SENSITIVE, INTELLIGENT,
OUTGOING

As man's oldest and most loyal friend in the animal kingdom, the dog, in all its varieties, plays a large part in the everyday life of the Chinese; from shepherds to ladies at court whose lapdogs live in the highest luxury. The most famous lapdogs, the Pekingese, are supposed to be descended from animals sent to the emperor as gifts from Constantine of Rome. The Chinese often call them 'lion-dogs'.

In astrology, the Dog is considered brave, loyal, intelligent, honest and open in all things. The Dog is not particularly ambitious for money or fame, but needs to feel useful and appreciated. The Dog is a good judge of character and is generally not easy to fool, but loyalty can blind it to the imperfections of superiors or family members.

The Dog is one of the Horse's best friends and most staunch allies. Together they make a formidable team. A year of the Dog is a good one in which to launch new enterprises, for the Horse will find unexpected support coming in from all sides.

Friends & Enemies

BOAR *Zhu*

CHEERFUL, SENSUAL, TOLERANT, GENEROUS

The Boar or Pig has been classed among the six main domestic animals in China since hunters first settled down to till the soil. The character for 'family' combines those for 'pig' and 'house', so the pig is a symbol of wealth and contentment. Pork is one of the favourite dishes, especially at New Year.

The Pig was one of Monkey's companions in his great quest for the Buddhist scriptures and was rewarded with a place as an Immortal in the Western Paradise.

People governed by the sign of the Boar are considered honest, reliable, cheerful and sociable. They generally strive less for power than domestic bliss, but are capable of leadership when necessary. Their best qualities show in times of crisis when they bring their full intelligence to bear on the problems. Otherwise they have a tendency to do only as much as is necessary for a good life.

The Horse and the Pig are opposite in many ways, the Pig loving domestic pleasures while the Horse is ever restless for new horizons – but both are honest, intelligent and sociable and enjoy each other's company for limited periods. In times of war they make natural allies but are quite happy to go their separate ways afterwards. Years of the Pig tend to benefit most signs but the Horse needs to take care not to rock the boat with wild ideas.

Chapter Four
Strengths and Weaknesses

WHEN THE WAY PREVAILS IN THE EMPIRE, SWIFT HORSES ARE RELEGATED TO PLOUGHING THE FIELDS;

WHEN THE WAY DOES NOT PREVAIL IN THE EMPIRE, WAR-HORSES BREED ON THE BORDERS.

LAO TZU *TAO TE CHING* 2:66

The beauty of Chinese astrology is that it is so simple to grasp the basic principles. Once you have a picture of what the twelve basic signs represent, it is a short step to arriving at a character sketch of yourself and others in those terms, and a basic idea of how well you are likely to relate. It is vastly simpler than Western astrology in which not only are there twelve signs, but also the planets, the moon and the stars which all have to be taken into account. Even given one's precise moment of birth it takes a fair grasp of the system's mathematics to arrive at a birth chart, and even more knowledge to draw any conclusions from it.

By contrast, in Chinese astrology your simple date of birth will give you a year and month sign. The year tells how you are most likely to respond to major events. It is your Yang, or outgoing aspect. It is the influence that you and everyone else born in that year acquires from the spirit of your times. Your month sign shows your Yin aspect, which is more personal. It shows how you relate in one to one dealings with others and how you personally will respond to what life throws your way. A simple glance at the Friends and Enemies chart on page 49 will show how comfortably these sit together and how straightforward or complex you are likely to find major decisions in life – whether you are often at odds with yourself or not.

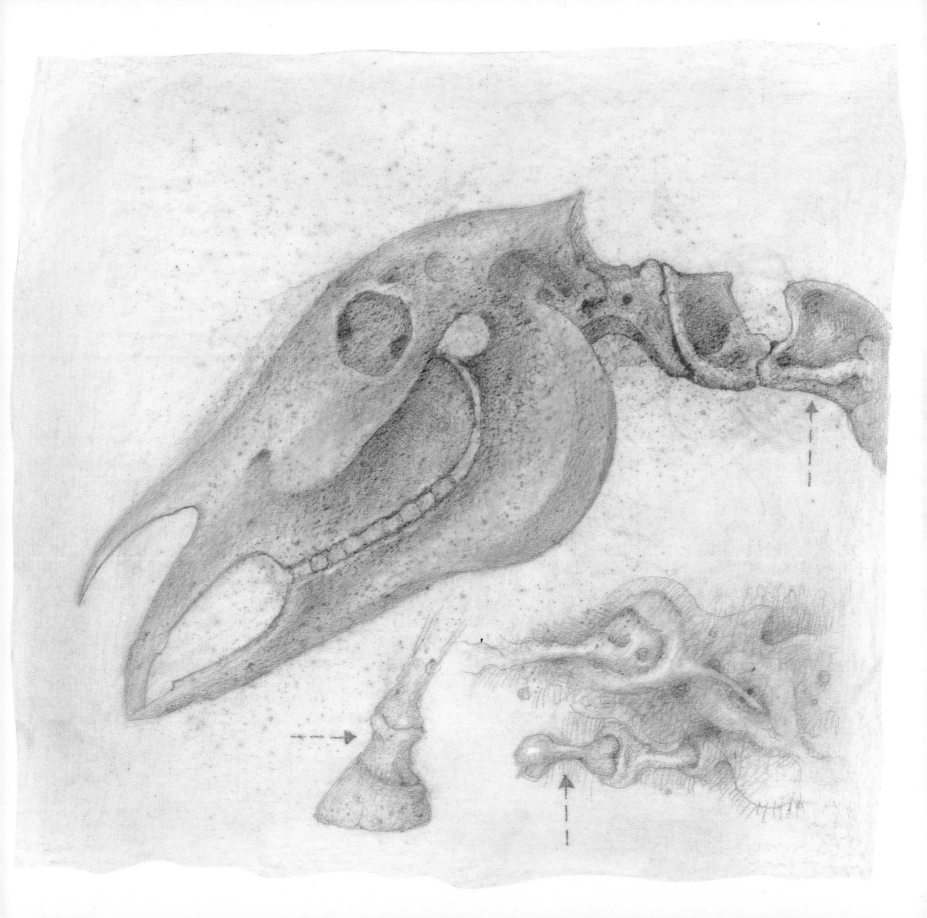

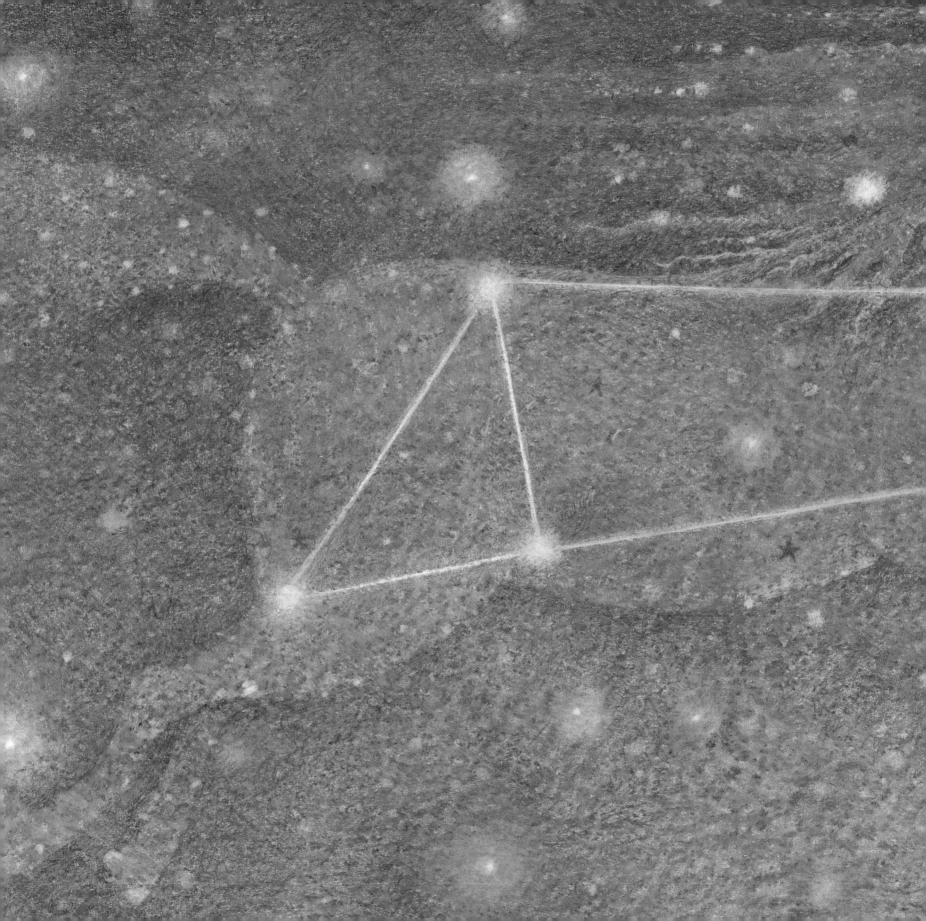

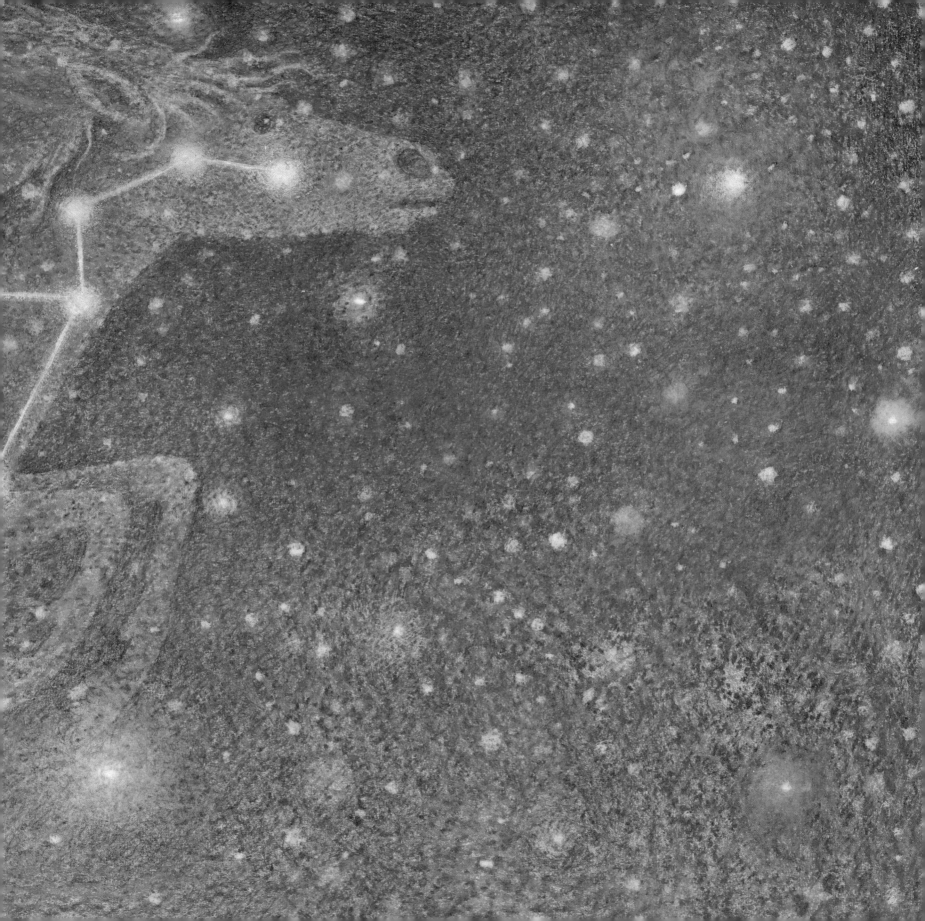

If you also happen to know the hour sign of your birth, this gives a third factor that can be entered in the Friends and Enemies chart; and although its effect will be more subtle than the other two, it may well explain certain secret yearnings and inclinations that you rarely voice, even to yourself, but which nevertheless affect your choices and reactions.

Without any awkward calculations, you now have a coherent picture of what Chinese astrology has to say about you. And from this it is a short step to take the birth signs of friends or colleagues or even organizations and see how they compare with your own – what clashes and harmonies there are on paper. You can then compare these with your experience of relating to those people, and this often seems startlingly accurate. It is also interesting to compare how smoothly or otherwise certain years run in relation to what astrology predicts in them for you.

Chinese astrology can be, and indeed often is, taken much further than this and by the end seems barely less complicated than Western astrology. In China, one can buy hefty almanacs that define the nature of each day of the year, and by relating that to their own profile, many Chinese will either begin or postpone major undertakings. They also use these almanacs to determine the nature of their day of birth and add that to their personal equation. But it is not necessary to take things that far. The beauty of Chinese astrology is the ease with which anyone can grasp its basic principles and test them out for themselves, without having to rely on the skill, sagacity and indeed trustworthiness of qualified practitioners.

For us, the attraction is also, as we mentioned earlier, that astrology opens a window into the Chinese soul. Whether it actually works is almost a secondary consideration. Because so many great minds have assumed that it does, and have applied themselves to refining the system, that is almost a justification in itself for studying it. As with the *I Qing*, the other great system of divination that holds an equally high place in Chinese culture, astrology is a distillation of how the Chinese view themselves and the world.

An essential part of Chinese philosophy, as evinced in astrology and elsewhere, is that it constantly aims towards reconciling and balancing opposites. There is much less emphasis on the need to conquer evil than in the West. Its existence is certainly recognized and given due respect, but it is seen not so much as a primal force of nature in itself as a by-product of imbalance between Yin and Yang or the elements. Rather than attempting to combat evil head on by means of virtue, the Chinese aim to root out its underlying causes. Get the balance right and evil will dissipate of its own accord, they say.

This is refreshing, if a bit puzzling at first, to Westerners like ourselves in whom it is ingrained from birth that good and evil form the most basic duality of all. Demons are certainly considered a very real menace in China, as we have seen by the care people take to guard their homes and tombs against them. There are also vivid depictions of hell and its administrators that would do justice to the wildest medieval European imaginations. But the

concept of evil is curiously absent, for example, from the Chinese account of the creation of the world. Also, good and evil are notably missing from the list of fundamental opposites in the table of Yin and Yang qualities below.

Rather than attempting to tackle evil head-on, as good Christians are taught, more emphasis is placed in China on understanding the Way or *Tao*, or its Buddhist equivalent, which is the secret pattern of harmony underlying the universe, than on grasping the nature of evil. In everyday practice the results are often not so different. Most Chinese have to strive as determinedly as any Christian to maintain their virtue and avoid slipping into evil or

destructive ways, but this end is reached by different means. It is noticeable in China how much more often people who are at odds will sit down to try and reconcile their differences rather than simply going to war over them. The opposites of Yin and Yang are seen as complementary. Neither side is meant to win over the other because that is what opens the way to evil.

Similarly, although each of the astrological signs has a negative aspect, they are all considered as good as each other, just different. One is not intrinsically better than the other. The Dragon is probably the most highly respected sign purely because of the

creature's overwhelming significance in China, but otherwise the signs are all pretty much equally respected. Westerners may baulk at being labelled a Rat, Snake or Pig, but to the Chinese these signs have as many virtues as, say, more obviously noble creatures like the Tiger or the Horse.

Some signs are natural enemies, but this is not to be seen as a disaster if you happen to have both in your birth profile. It just means you may have to work harder to reconcile them than people whose birth signs happen to be in perfect natural harmony. It can even be a blessing to be forced to accommodate opposite tendencies.

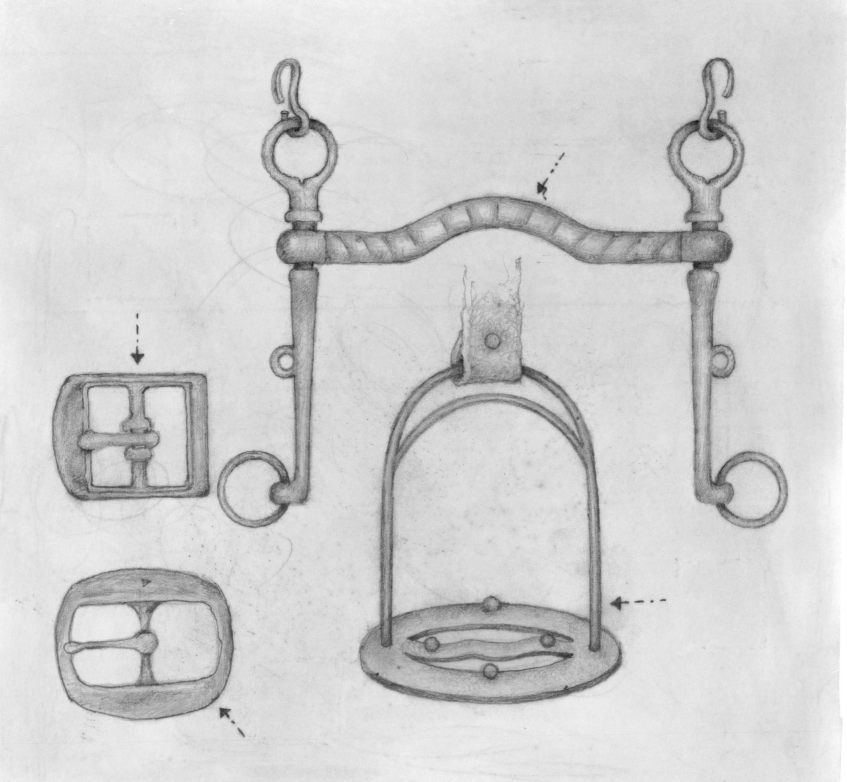

Yin and Yang

The Way begets One; One begets Two;
Two begets Three;
Three begets the myriad creatures.
The myriad creatures bear
on their backs the Yin
and embrace in their arms the Yang
and are the blending of the
generative forces of the two.

LAO TZU *TAO TE CHING* 2:42

The concept of the interplay between Yin and Yang is as basic to Chinese philosophy as that of the Five Elements. Even more basic, in fact, because they say that the very first thing to come into existence when the universe was just formless chaos was the Cosmic Egg, which was simply Yin and Yang in their most pure form. To this day, this is represented by the ubiquitous black and white disc representing perfect balance. Only later did the Five Elements, the Four Most Fortunate Creatures and all the rest come into being.

The Yin-Yang disc is an emblem of both the start and end of creation. It is an ideal of harmony towards which all creation aspires and which in practice is rarely achieved more than fleetingly. Nevertheless, the constant striving towards that perfect harmony and balance is what has always preoccupied China's sages.

Table of Opposites

Yin	Yang
Moon	Sun
Earth	Sky
Matter	Spirit
Dark	Light
Female	Male
Passive	Active
Receptive	Creative
Down	Up
Water	Fire
Winter	Summer

The sun and moon are the essence
Of primal Yang and primal Yin
Because Heaven must know
what happens in the world.
It created the sun and moon
For the endless toil
of coursing across the sky
Serving as Heaven's eyes and
pouring down light.
If these eyes are obscured when
the Lord of Heaven walks the Way
By what shall he set his course?

LU TUNG (C. AD 800)

As in any society, ideals are often far removed from everyday practice in China. Despite it being repeated over and over in the philosophies that Yin and Yang are equal and complementary, in everyday life the Yang qualities are usually considered preferable. Men are given preference over women, summer appreciated more than winter and so on. This, say the sages, is why the Empire constantly falls short of perfection and is periodically overtaken by discord and war. However, this is probably no more the case in China than in any other part of the world, in fact, in China, people go to extraordinary lengths of politeness to avoid arguments and disputes, and this must have something to do with the pervasive influence of their philosophy of balancing opposites.

Strengths and Weaknesses